Muhammad Ali

The Illustrated Biography

Muhammad Ali

The Illustrated Biography

CHRISTINE KIDNEY

Photographs by

Daily Mail

Welcome Rain Publishers   New York

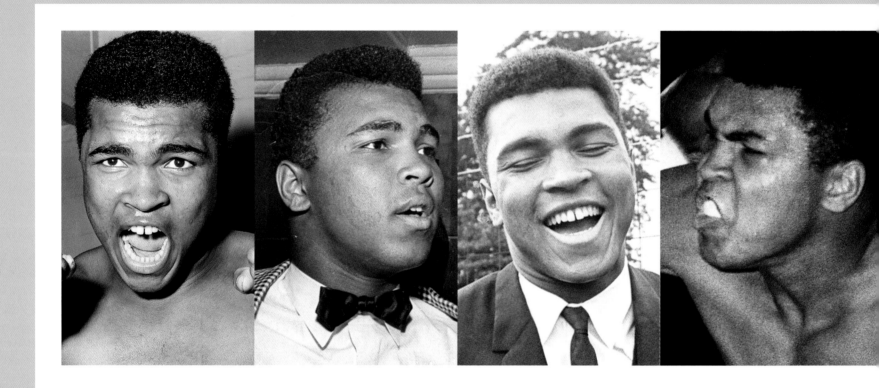

This Edition Published by Welcome Rain Publishers LLC in 2009

First published by
Transatlantic Press
38 Copthorne Road
Croxley Green, Hertfordshire
WD3 4AQ, UK

Text © Transatlantic Press
For photographs see page 224

ISBN 1-56649-997-6 / 978-1-56649-997-2

Printed in Malaysia

Contents

Introduction   6

Part One   Pursuing a Dream   8

Part Two   Heavyweight Champion
              of the World   50

Part Three   Back in the Ring   116

Part Four   I'm Just Getting Started   194

Chronology   220

Acknowledgments   224

Introduction

Muhammad Ali first came into the public eye when, as Cassius Clay, he won a gold medal at the Olympic Games in Rome in 1960. He would become the greatest boxer the world has ever seen but at the height of his career, at a critical turning point in the history of America, he was prepared to take a political stance that nearly ruined his career.

In 1964 he stunned the boxing community with his defeat of Sonny Liston, the heavyweight champion, to take the title for the first time. Only those closest to Clay knew that he had the speed and the ability to outfox even the greatest punch in the history of boxing, which is precisely what he did. Throughout his extraordinary career, his influence on the world of boxing changed the sport forever.

Muhammad Ali, The Illustrated Biography charts the life of this fascinating and complex man through a series of amazing action photographs, as well as powerful and intimate images of Ali at rest or on the public stage. While the photographs shot during the fights show the raw power, athleticism and skill of the fighter they are balanced by portrayals of his humanity and wit.

The photographs, drawn from the *Daily Mail*'s comprehensive archive, are accompanied by detailed captions which add context and depth to give a rounded and comprehensive portrait of the man who truly is 'The Greatest'.

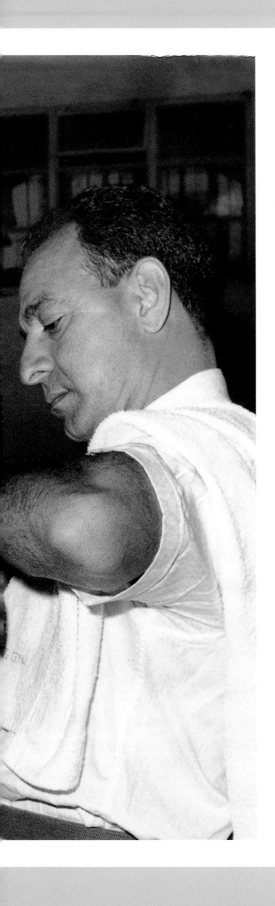

Part One

Pursuing a Dream

Olympic champion

Above: Eighteen-year-old Cassius Clay proudly bears his Olympic gold medal in 1960. This relatively unknown boxer beat Pole Zbigniew Pietrzykowski (to Clay's left) into second place. Despite being welcomed home as a national hero, the Olympic champion was still refused a coffee in a whites-only café in his native Louisville, Kentucky. And in the minds of many sports commentators, he still had much to prove among the ranks of the champions.

Opposite: An early photograph of the 'loudmouth' who would win over the hearts of millions across the world. From a very early age Cassius Clay knew the value of publicity and was a sportswriter's dream. His effusive self-promotion charmed some and irritated others but they always had something to write about. It also helped ticket sales. Behind the scenes, Clay was an extremely disciplined athlete.

Under contract

Opposite: Clay was early on signed up by the Louisville Group, a group of 11 of white businessmen. The contract gave him 50 per cent of any earnings, with the Group paying for costs out of their 50 per cent, and 15 per cent of Clay's income put aside into a pension fund. This irritated Clay but was a generous and considerate act, given that many boxers were thrown on the scrap heap after retiring.

Above: A publicity shot for the fight that was to take place in June 1963 between Clay and the British Heavyweight Champion, Henry Cooper, at London's Wembley Arena. Despite the inevitable partisanship towards 'our 'Enery', the London press and public were fascinated by Clay. Soon after the fight, Columbia records released an album entitled *The Greatest, a celebration by Cassius Clay* – in poems and monologues – of Cassius Clay.

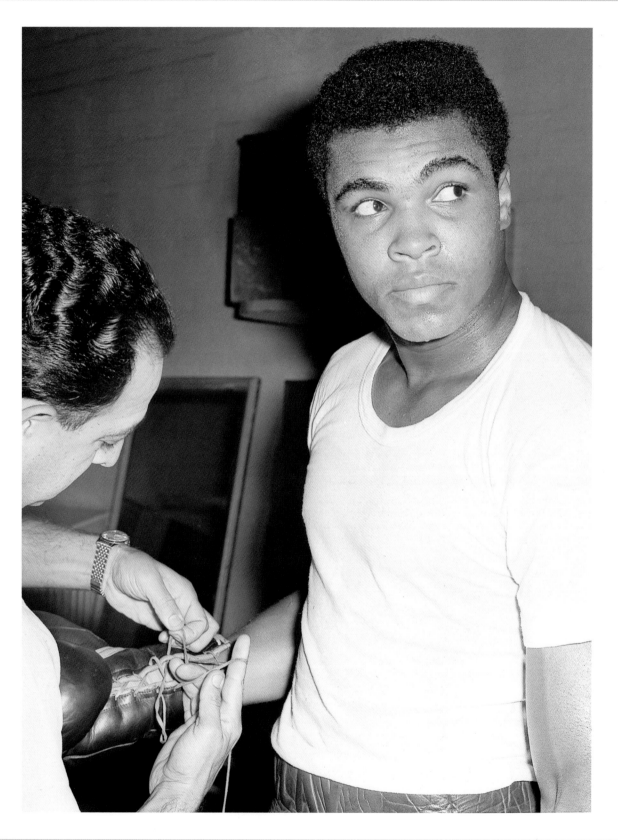

Family matters

Opposite: Cassius Clay striring pancake mix at home in Louisville with his younger brother Rudolph looking on, before their departure for the Cooper fight in London. The Clay brothers were born into relative comfort, though, along with all other blacks in the south, suffered the injustices of segregation. Their mother Odessa cleaned and cooked for a white family and their father Cassius Clay Snr was a sign painter.

Left: Angelo Dundee laces Clay's gloves. Dundee (born Angelo Mirena) was the first trainer who had not tried to mould Clay to his own style. Later, Ali was to say: 'He never bosses me, tells me when to run, how much to box. I do what I want to do. I'm free.' Dundee in turn said of Clay: 'I learned this ... if a guy's a short guy make him shorter, if he's tall make him taller.'

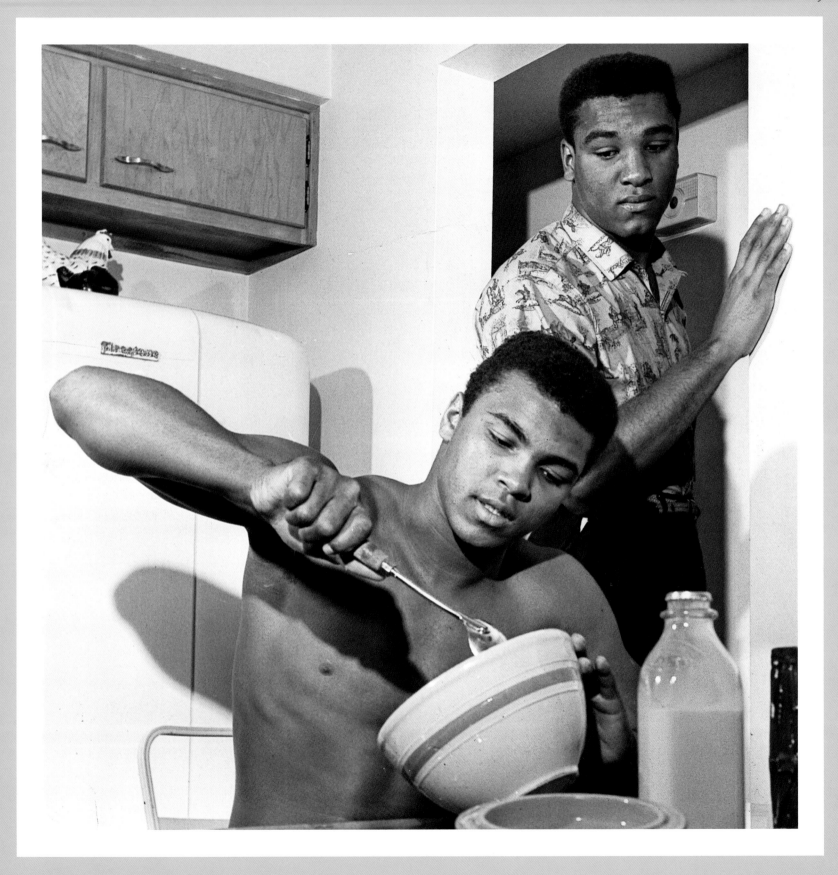

Something to declare

Opposite: When Cassius Clay arrived in London, he was asked in Customs, along with every other passenger about to walk through Arrivals, whether he had anything to declare. This was gift of a question to Clay, who proceeded to bemuse and amuse the officials with predictions of his win against Cooper in five rounds. Here he wields the fist that will finish the job.

Right: Clay, perhaps tongue in cheek, sports the then uniform of the city gent, complete with bowler, spats and umbrella. His playfulness would often mislead other competitors – notoriously Sonny Liston – into underestimating his seriousness and threat as a fighter. It was often a deliberate ploy as well as a naturally irrepressible sense of fun. He pronounced Buckingham Palace a 'swell pad'.

Just sparring

Opposite: Cassius Clay with a young sparring partner. Clay was famously generous with his time for the public, notably in the case of children. He would stress the importance of clean living and nutrition, advising children to keep away from candy and sweet drinks.

Left: Soon after arriving in London, Clay walks through Picadilly with the Clay–Cooper fight promoter, Jack Solomons. Clay had come to London on a popularity-boosting exercise. He had recently fought Doug Jones at New York's Madison Square Garden and only just beaten him, despite predicting that he would win in four rounds. It lasted ten and Clay won on points. The public and sportswriters seemed set to turn against the 'loudmouth'.

Making a prediction

Opposite: Once again, Clay predicts at a press conference the number of rounds it will take to knock Cooper out. Clay was also squaring up for a fight against Sonny Liston and took every opportunity to bait the 'big ugly bear'. He stated that 'all heavyweights fighting today are bums and cripples – and that goes for that big ugly bear, Liston. He may be great, but he falls in eight.' Cooper quipped after their fight, 'We didn't do so bad for a "bum" and a "cripple", did we?'

Above: With sparring partner Jimmy Ellis on his right, and Cooper and Solomons in the background, Clay is inviting Ingemar Johansson, Cooper and Brian London to fight him in the ring at the same time, adding that he'll take them all out in nine rounds. Cooper takes Clay's posturing in good humour.

Stopping to chat

Opposite: Clay in training with his sparring partner Jimmy Ellis, on Lower Regent Street in London. Despite the early hour of the day, a number of sports journalists had witnessed the great athlete exercising in Hyde Park. Clay and Ellis still had time to chat and joke with people on their way to work. One passenger on a bus called out to him, asking who he was. He replied, 'I'm Sonny Liston.'

Above: Clay and his companion Dave Edgar talk to a policeman on the beat at Picadilly Circus.

Training with Dundee

Opposite: Angelo Dundee laces Clay's gloves as Clay begins some serious training in the run-up to his fight with Cooper. Ferdie Pacheco, Clay's physician, said of Dundee: 'He was ... strong when he needed to be strong and weak when he needed to be weak ... Angelo was always, always subservient to the fighter. He was never ego-maniacal like most of these managers ...'

Above: Clay often trained in front of an audience, whether invited or members of the public walking in off the street. Here he spars with his younger brother Rudolph. Rudolph often travelled with him, later becoming his companion and driver.

Dressed to impress

Left: Clay arrived at the weigh-in wearing an outlandish red robe, which he had had made in London, for a grand £35. He later wore it into the ring on the night of the fight, set off by a fetching imitation of the British crown. Cooper, in modest contrast, wore a brown cardigan over his shorts at the weigh-in.

Opposite: On the off-chance that anyone has missed his prediction, Clay announces the number of rounds it will take to knock out the man whose hand he is shaking. Again, Cooper takes it in good humour. Clay weighed in at 207lbs, Cooper at 185 1/2lbs. Clay annoyed many British fans, who by now saw Cooper as the underdog. Unphased, Cooper smiled and said, 'I'll give him a good fight.'

Cooper v Clay

Opposite and right: Watched and driven on by 55,000 Englishmen, Cooper constantly jabs at Clay for four rounds. Clay is almost unhurt, while Cooper is injured and bleeding. Clay constantly flirts with the audience, and plays cat and mouse with Cooper. Just as Cooper is about to fall, Clay steps back and shows off to the audience, carried away with his own prediction of finishing in five, not any earlier. One of his American sponsors, William Faversham, warned him to 'stop the funny business'.

Legend has it that Clay's attention was distracted by the delectable Elizabeth Taylor who was sitting in the front row. This gave Cooper the opportunity for a punch that dazed Clay and landed him on his backside, nearly losing him the fight as well as his dignity.

Fight stopped

Left and opposite: Before round four had finished, Clay managed to get back on his feet. His trainer, Angelo Dundee, had spotted an opportunity that would save the fight for Clay: a small tear in one of his gloves. This was brought to the attention of the referee and in the minute it took to find a replacement pair, Clay regained his composure. Clay fought Cooper unrelentingly for the next two minutes, when the referee stopped the fight.

Young love

Left: Clay with his first wife, Sonji, in London. Cassius's first girlfriend Areatha Swint, wrote in a memoir, 'I was the first girl he ever kissed, and he didn't know how. So I had to teach him. When I did, he fainted. Really, he just did. He was always joking, so I thought he was playing, but he fell so hard.' He and Sonji were deeply in love but the Nation of Islam was to come between them.

Opposite: After the Cooper fight, Sonny Liston's manager visited Clay in his dressing room. Liston had finally agreed to fight him. Here Clay begins his psychological campaign against Liston – he had defeated Cooper in five rounds, and would get Liston in eight. Clay said later of the lead-up to the fight, 'I set out to make him think ... that I was some clown ... I didn't want nobody thinking nothing except that I was a joke.'

Nation of Islam

Clay waits to be taken to the airport to fly home and start training for the Liston fight in Las Vegas. This was the fight he had been waiting for since beginning his professional career. For some time he had been talking to the leaders of the Nation of Islam, who preached black separatism rather than the integration of Martin Luther King. Clay kept this out of the press as much as possible, aware that it would damage the public's appetite for the Liston fight.

Above: Cassius and his brother Rudolph chat to Norma Lindon and Brenda Howell in their hotel lounge.

Preparing for the Liston fight

Opposite: Liston was the most powerful boxer that Clay had ever fought and so he took his training very seriously. In addition, as part of the psychological campaign, Clay bought a 30-passenger red and white bus, on which he painted a sign that read, 'World's Most Colorful Fighter: Liston must go in eight.' He once parked it outside Liston's house and called the local press. In contrast, Liston was living what Clay described as the 'rich, fat ritual of the champ'.

Above: A week before the fight, Clay spars before onlookers, many of whom would have walked in off the street and paid a small fee to watch.

A visit from the Fab Four

Opposite and above: Beatlemania had begun to take America by storm and Harold Conrad – one of the promoters of the Clay–Liston fight – saw a press opportunity in staging an introduction between these men who would one day become iconic figures of the twentieth century. Conrad had rejected Liston's participation after the latter said, 'My dog plays drums better than that kid with the big nose.'

Heavyweight weigh-in

Above: Clay holds up eight fingers – a prediction that he will win in the eighth round. At the weigh-in Clay staged a mock attack on Liston. Malcolm X, who spent a lot of time with Clay in the lead-up to the fight, observed of his friend's tactics: 'I suspected ... that he was doing everything possible to con and to 'psyche' Sonny Liston into coming into the ring angry, poorly trained, and overconfident.' Liston was a graduate of the school of hard knocks: unpopular with the public, he was an ex-con whose only chance of redemption was sponsorship by the mob.

Opposite: Odessa and Cassius Clay Snr. Clay Snr had let the cat out of the bag to the press about Clay's imminent conversion to Islam, complaining that the Nation of Islam had taken his son's money.

Clay v Liston

Opposite and above: Clay and Liston fought on February 25, 1964. Liston's immense power was no match for Clay's speed. By the third round, Liston was tiring. Towards the end of the fourth round, Clay's eyes began to sting until he could barely see. Cynics thought that Liston's gloves had been coated with a substance to hurt Clay's eyes, but it was most likely either the coagulant on Liston's cuts or the liniment on his shoulder that got on to Clay's gloves. When Clay then brushed the sweat away from his forehead, the substance got on to his skin and mixed in with the perspiration dripping into his eyes. Clay was about to stop the fight, but Dundee washed his eyes out before round five.

Clay triumphs

Above: For the first four rounds, until his eyes began to smart, Clay had done a good job of outwitting Liston and tiring him out. By the time his eyes had cleared at the beginning of the sixth round, he didn't need to hold back. Clay later recalled, 'I hit him with eight punches in a row, until he doubled up.'

Opposite: Liston quit, sitting on his stool, after round six. Clay's response was triumph over the commentators and sportswriters who had doubted him: 'I am the king! I am the king! King of the world! Eat your words! Eat your words!' Not all of them did, yet. The mode of Liston's defeat had not proved Clay's supremacy in many eyes.

An emotional evening

Above: Clay goes off in victory to talk to the press, with Drew 'Bundini' Brown behind him shedding tears of joy. For many years, Bundini was Clay's motivator – strange, comical and very empathetic: 'I get sick before a fight. It makes me feel like a pregnant woman. I give the champ all my strength. He throw a punch, I throw a punch. He get hit, it hurts me.'

Opposite: Clay poses for a shot with his belt over his shoulder. Although he had tried to keep his conversion out of the press, the notice on the wall seems to indicate that he is already a Muslim.

Announcing his conversion

Opposite: After winning the Heavyweight title from Sonny Liston, Clay was now free to announce his conversion to Islam and his membership of the Nation of Islam, led by Elijah Muhammad, who had cut off Malcolm X. Ali's support of the Nation of Islam was a great blow to his friend Malcolm X, whose increasing moderation was now converging with the views of the great civil rights leader, Martin Luther King.

Above: Three months after the fight, Ali travelled to Africa for a month-long tour, partly to cool off all the bad publicity he had received after his conversion. Here he visits the Hussein Mosque in Cairo.

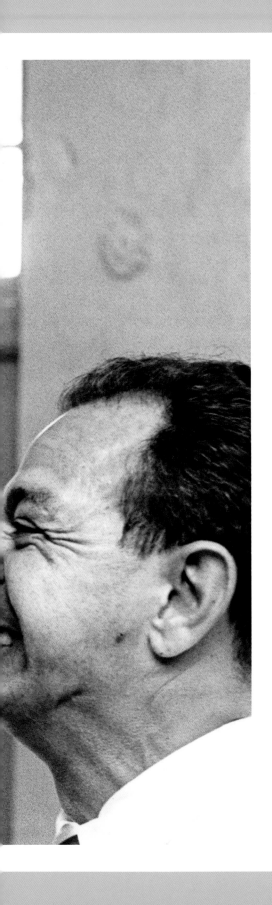

Part Two

Heavyweight Champion of the World

Float like a butterfly

Opposite: One of the most famous catchphrases ever is emblazoned on the back of Bundini Brown's T-shirt, pictured during a training session at the Fifth Street Gym in Miami. Bundini and Ali shouted it at the infamous weigh-in before the first Liston fight. It is still the phrase most associated with Ali, embodying his speed, his wit and his precision.

Right: Ali visited the Sea World Aquarium while training in Miami. The dolphin seems unphased by Ali's threat. The champion observes, 'It looks like I finally met someone with a bigger mouth than me.'

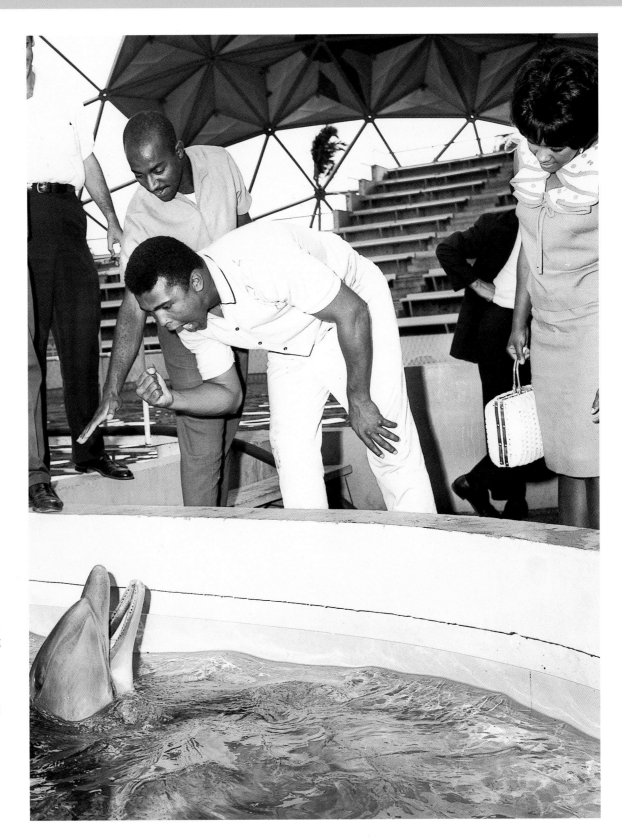

Rematch with Liston

Above: A rematch against Liston was scheduled in Boston for three months after the first. This time Liston trained hard. as he had early in his career. Just before the fight, Ali was rushed to hospital with a hernia that could have threatened his life. The fight was postponed until May 1965. On hearing the news, Liston is said to have cracked open a bottle of vodka and made himself a screwdriver – he knew that he would not be able to maintain the level of fitness he had attained. Ali knocked him out in the first round.

Opposite: The referee Joe Walcott famously forgot to start the count in his attempts to move Ali away from Liston. Ali at the time didn't think he had hit Liston very hard: 'I wanted to whup him bad. I didn't want him making excuses, or quitting.'

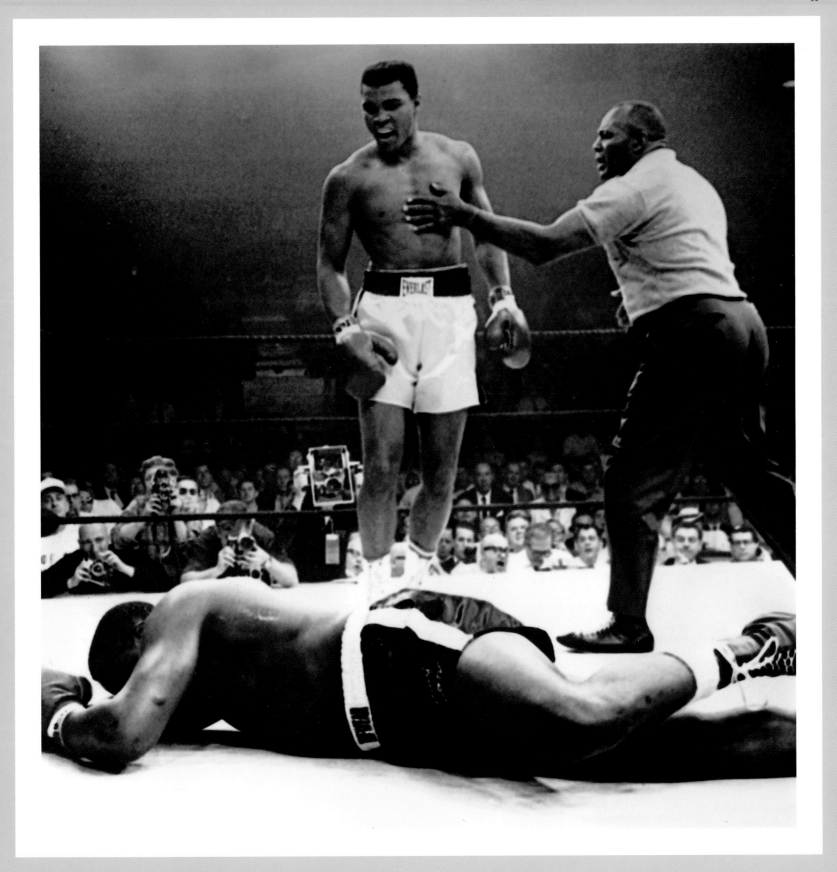

Voted 'Fighter of the Year'

Left and opposite: Many still believe that Liston took a dive in the second Ali fight, although Liston's widow Geraldine always denied it. Liston himself refused ever to speak about it. Both fights had been shrouded in controversy and sportswriters expressed polar opinions on Ali's abilities. Added to this was Ali's unpopular membership of the Nation of Islam. So it came as some surprise when Ali was awarded the Edward J Neil Fighter of the Year trophy 1965.

Patterson challenges for the title

Opposite and above: Floyd Patterson challenged Ali to the title in November 1965. Patterson had yearned for acceptance by white American society in a way that Ali, and to some extent Liston, had not. He took it upon himself very publicly as a Christian to fight Ali as a Black Muslim, a boxing crusade. Patterson, near the end of his career, was not in Ali's league. Although the fight reached twelve rounds, this was largely because Ali held back. The press criticized him for this, to which Ali's response was, understandably: 'If I knock him out fast, you'd say it was fixed. If I knock him out slow, I'm a brute.'

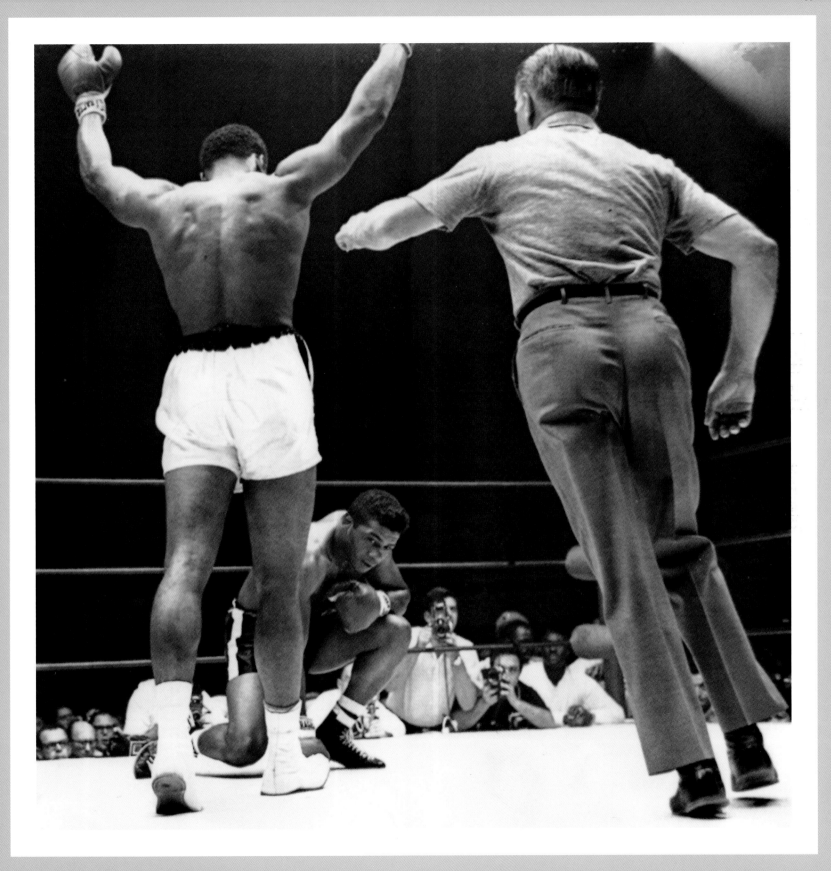

'I ain't got no quarrel with them Vietcong'

Opposite: Ali arrives to a warm reception in London in May 1966 to defend his title against Henry Cooper. It had become almost impossible for Ali to fight in America, as his unpopularity was making backers lose money on his fights. Ali was in the middle of a political storm back at home, as he was resisting the draft to go and fight in the escalating war in Vietnam. He quipped to the press, 'I ain't got no quarrel with them Vietcong', a phrase that would later go some way into making him an American hero.

Above: Ali jumping fences in a London park – showing what a considerable athlete he was.

Cooper bids for world title

Left: Ali and British Heavyweight Champion Henry Cooper at the press conference for the fight. This was Cooper's last attempt at the title. He was thirty-two, Ali only twenty-four.It was also a major sporting event for England, especially as Ali's fame had spread beyond the ring into the realms of celebrity. Cooper had almost knocked Ali out in their first fight, so hopes were high on the home ground.

Opposite: Ali and Cooper pose with good humour. Ali wasn't chanting predictions of knocking Cooper out and was relatively subdued. He even paid Cooper a compliment in saying the British heavyweight had hit him the hardest in a fight.

Away from the ring

Above: Ali leaving the London Free School in Notting Hill in London, where he talked to children and signed autographs. He visited at the behest of Michael X, a black British Muslim who led the Racial Adjustment Society, the closest thing Britain had to the Nation of Islam. Here he stands at the top of the steps, listening to the crowds cheer and jeer him. An avenue of bodyguards from the Racial Adjustment Society flank his way out.

Opposite: Ali leaves the Picadilly Hotel to go for a walk in the streets of London. In contrast to his visit to the London Free School, Ali is alone, unprotected by bodyguards. This was how he preferred to be, saying that no one would be able to stop a determined assassin, and that Allah was watching over him. Ali's stature (6 foot 3 inches) is even more noticeable when he is seen next to the average man and woman in the street.

Taking a break

Above: Ali and Jimmy Ellis, his sparring partner, take a break from training in Hyde Park in London. The corgi seems indifferent to Ali's insistence that he pick up the ball.

Left: The faithful Angelo Dundee tapes Ali's hands during training before the Cooper fight. Ali trained in the west of London, in White City, while Cooper was based at the Thomas à Becket gym on the Old Kent Road in south-east London.

Training injuries

Left: Ali rests during training. He had been having problems with his hands, which kept bleeding during training. Referring to previous fights, including the one against Patterson, he said, 'The hardest thing I hit for those fights was my opponents. I just had to stop punching the bag. I had a lot of pain. My hands were bleeding after every training session.'

Opposite: Angelo Dundee had helped Ali keep the problems with his hands out of the press. Here they share a joke while Dundee tries to fix Ali's head protector for a sparring session. Some of the Muslims around Ali were convinced that Dundee was trying to bring Ali down, but Dundee let most of that wash over him.

Concientious objector

Opposite and above: Ali spars in preparation for the Cooper match. Two days before the fight, on May 21, 1966, both Ali and Cooper left their gyms and used road work and general exercise to build stamina and speed. During all this time, Ali was waiting to hear from America to see whether he had been granted 'conscientious objector' status in relation to his stance on Vietnam. HIs commitment to training was unparalleled, and so too was his commitment to his political beliefs outside the ring.

Medical checks

Opposite and right: Dr Paul Saville of the British Boxing Board of Control does some medical checks on Ali before the fight. 'Both boxers were fit as a fiddle,' he said. He also said he had never seen Cooper so fit, which must have been encouraging for the fans of the British challenger.

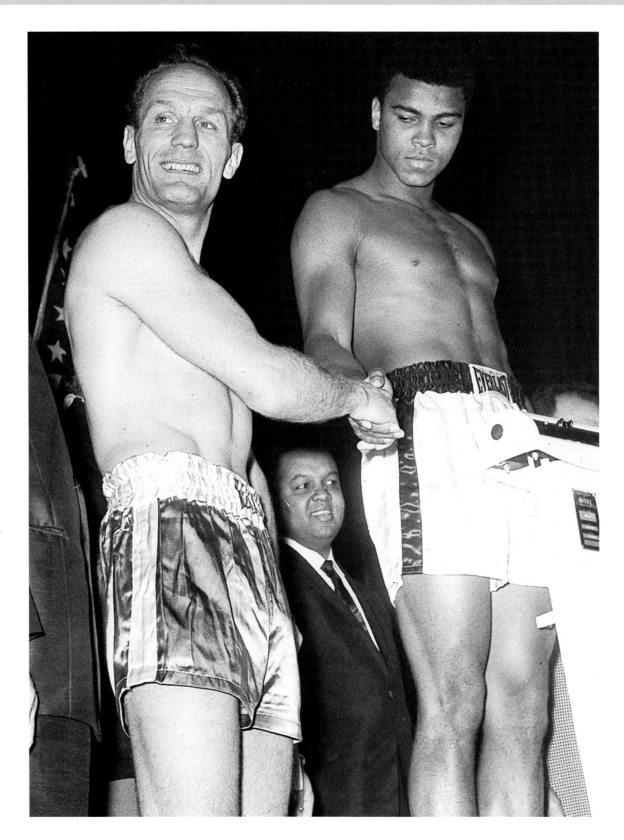

A sporting contest

Opposite: The venue for the London fight, Arsenal's Highbury Stadium, had already sold out on its seats, leaving 8,000 tickets for standing only. The weigh-in took place 12 hours before the fight. Ali was at his lightest, 201 1/2 lbs; Cooper was nearly 3 lbs heavier, at 188 lbs, than when they had last met in 1963.

Right: The two men display genuine sportsmanship. Cooper has recently said that Ali wasn't just boxing, he was History, and that he feels privileged to have played a small part in that history.

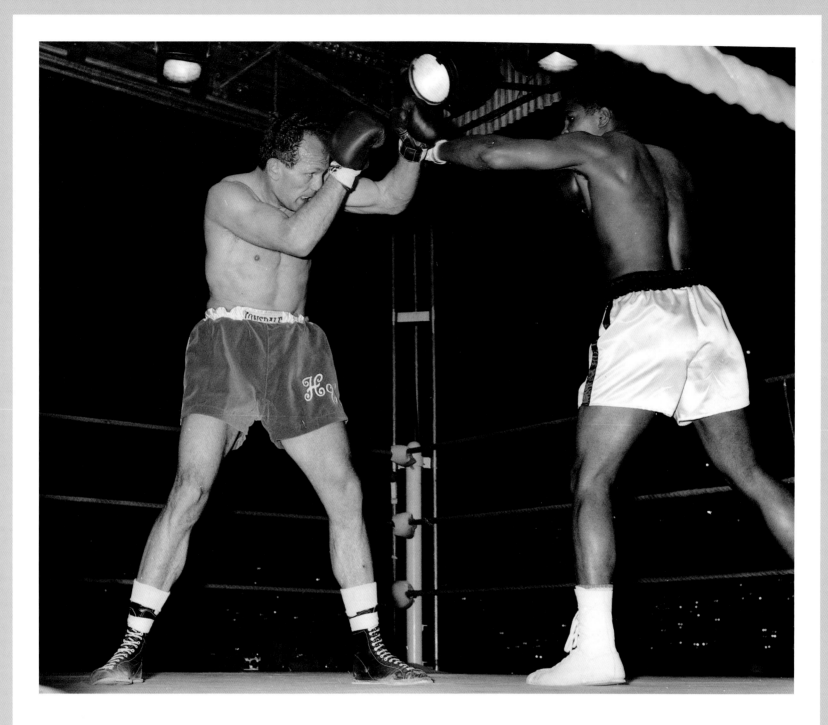

An international audience

Above and opposite: In the end, 45,000 people squeezed into Highbury to see the fight; 30,000 saw it on 'pay television' and 20 million viewers watched it on satellite back in America. Cooper put up a good fight, even though Ali outclassed him. Cooper's age wasn't his only disadvantage: his sparring partner had not matched the speed with which Ali would come at him.

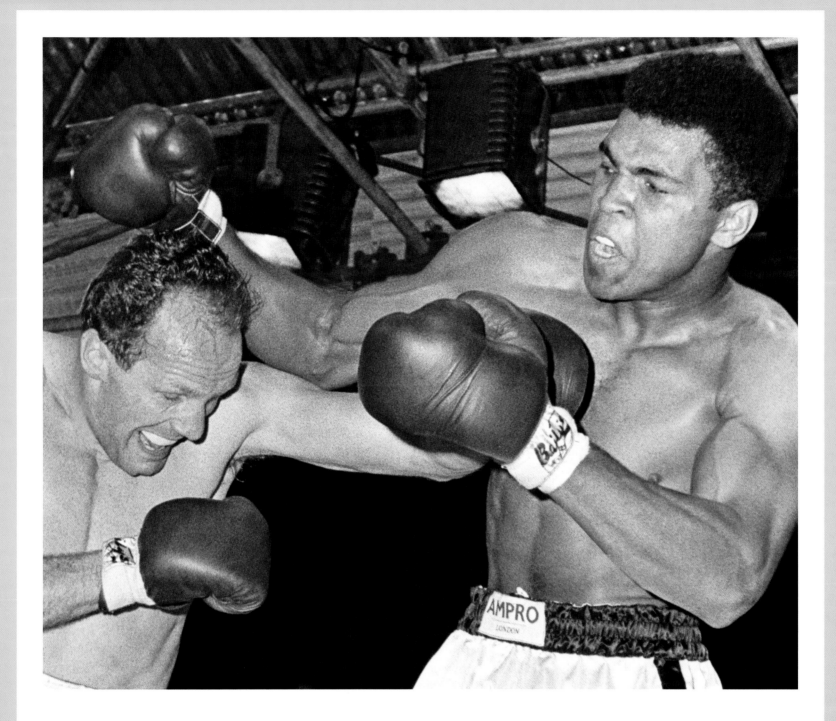

Stopped in the sixth

Opposite: Henry's left hook – ''Enry's Ammer' – failed to land most of the time, although he did make contact with a few lefts and rights. These failed to mark Ali, as usual. Cooper's reach was yet another disadvantage to add to his tally, shown clearly here.

Above: By the sixth round, Ali had opened up an old cut above Cooper's eye, which started bleeding excessively. Years of boxing had worn the skin thin. It was Ali who suggested to the referee that the fight be stopped.

A man of many talents

Above: After the Cooper fight, Ali, looking unscathed, attended a press conference at the Picadilly Hotel. Here he plays the piano for the assembled journalists. As he had left the ring, four members of the audience had shouted racial abuse at him but Ali shrugged it off.

Opposite: The fight promoter Harry Levene tells the assembled press that the gross earnings from the fight were £400,000. Ali's share of this was £215,000, Cooper's £40,000.

Feeling the pressure

Opposite: Ali returned to London in August 1966 to fight Brian London. He was beginning to get jaded, even saying, 'There just ain't no more fun in it. There's nothing new and I'm used to it like going to work. It's the guys trying to beat me who get the most fun.' It was suggested that London would fight dirty. Ali responded, 'If London wants to fight dirty anything he does wrong I can do wrong.'

Above: Ali watches a private showing in the West End of the film of his fight with Cooper. These were subdued times for Ali, as the political storm clouds were gathering. He knew that at some point in the near future a decision would be made about his eligibility for the draft back in America.

An all-round entertainer

Above: Ali talks to Eamonn Andrews, the host of a popular British chat show. Ali has joined the ranks of the glitterati; the other guests on stage include Lucille Ball, Noel Coward and Dudley Moore.

Opposite: Ali looks through swatches of fabric to select one for his new suit to be tailored by Harry Helman. Standing over him is Herbert Muhammad, the son of Elijah Muhammad, the founder of the Nation of Islam. Herbert would soon become Ali's official agent, though he had been that in all but name for some time.

Visiting Egypt

Above: Soon after his fight with Cooper in London, Ali travelled to Egypt once more, this time at the invitation of the Supreme Council of Islamic Affairs. Ali began to develop a passion for Africa, which reached a crescendo during his fight in Zaire against George Foreman in the following decade.

Opposite: On his second trip to London in 1966, Ali visited the top of the Post Office Tower, from where he surveyed the city whose affection he was already conquering.

On set

Ali took time out of training for the Brian London fight to visit a friend of his, Jim Brown (above), on
the film set of *The Dirty Dozen*. The film was being filmed at Beechwood Park School in Markyate,
Hertfordshire. Lee Marvin (opposite) shows Ali the automatic weapon he uses in the movie.

Two fights on his mind

Left: Ali's disenchantment with the sport is beginning to show. He is attending a press conference for the Brian London fight in August 1966, but another fight is scheduled against Karl Mildenberger for the September. He said, 'I've got two fights in my mind and no heavyweight of the world should have that. I don't want to burn myself up.' He also knew he was treading water before he had to face the music back home.

Opposite: Ali during training. He took preparation for the fight very seriously, even though London was Britain's no 2 heavyweight.

A hard way to make a living

Left: Ali goes running in Hyde Park, with Stuart Denny, one of the managers of the Cumberland Hotel, where he is staying. He told reporters during one of his public sessions in the ring, 'I was up this morning at five, running for miles and miles. I wish I'd seen a doctor on television when I was a boy, instead of a boxer. This is a hard way to make a living. I'm getting old.'

Opposite: The press get a chance to see the magnificent athlete in training. Although not complacent, Ali did not rate London highly as a boxer.

Preparing to fight London

Opposite: Ali swerves out of the way with lightning speed as his favourite sparring partner, Jimmy Ellis, throws a straight left. They worked out for five rounds at the Noble Art Gym owned by the British Boxing Board of Control. Despite his low expectations of London's ability, Ali's training was intense, including pounding a heavy punch bag for the equivalent of five rounds, and choosing another sparring partner who moved in the same way as London.

Left: Ali poses for a publicity shot.

Mutual respect

Above: Ali called Cooper a gentleman, and takes time out of training to greet his former opponent. After his defeat of Cooper, he had gone to the loser's dressing room to apologize for the cut above Cooper's eye. Cooper said to Ali: 'It was a pity. We was really enjoying ourselves. But I would have done the same to you if I could!'

Opposite: Ali and Brian London shake hands at the weigh-in, with the fight promoter Jack Solomons standing between them.

Weighing in

Opposite: Ali weighed in at 209 1/2 lbs. He was eight pounds heavier than he had been when he'd fought Cooper. London weighed in at 200 1/2 lbs.

Right: The fight was broadcast live on BBC radio and was shown on live television in America. In Britain viewing was only available in cinemas. London is outclassed from the very beginning.

'More than the greatest'

Opposite and above: In the three rounds it took Ali to defeat London, the Briton took a hammering. Later he said, 'I went into the ring expecting to go the full 15 rounds. I reckon I'm as good as the rest. But Ali is different. He's more than the greatest. Everything happened so quickly; I don't know what punch actually got me.'

Ali stands back

Left: Ali stands back when London hits the floor and the referee Harry Gibb begins the count. London visited Ali in his dressing room after the fight to congratulate him, offering him the compliment, 'I'd like a return match, but only if you put a 56lb weight on each ankle.'

Opposite: Ali on his way to the airport after the London fight. He is due to appear before a special hearing regarding his conscientious objector status. The judge at the hearing recommended that Ali be exempted on account of his religious beliefs. Much of the public found Ali's pacifism unpalatable, given his chosen career.

Ali meets a hero

Ali shakes hands with Karl Mildenberger in Frankfurt in September 1966. Former champion Joe Louis stands between them. Joe Louis was a hero of Ali's, though for a long time Louis was vociferous in his disapproval of the company Ali was keeping in the Nation of Islam. They were later reconciled, and Ali was very generous to Louis. After Louis died, Ali said, 'Howard Hughes dies, with all his billions, not a tear. Joe Louis, everybody cried.'

Opposite: At the weigh-in, Karl Mildenberger checks Ali's weight. The fight went to 12 rounds, and Ali won on a technical decision. Mildenberger was gracious in defeat: 'I fought my best ... when he put me down in the tenth, that was when I knew I was in serious trouble.'

A generous gesture

Opposite: The referee Teddy Waltham leads Mildenberger to his corner after the final decision. Waltham was paid in cash by the promoters but unfortunately his pocket was picked. Ali got to hear about it and with typical generosity gave Waltham the amount he'd lost. He was known for his generous gestures: when Joe Louis was retired and eking out a tired existence on his former reputation, Ali brought him to his training camp and gave him $30,000.

Right: Ali stands in victory over Cleveland 'Big Cat' Williams. This was Ali's first fight in a year on American soil. Williams wasn't much of an opponent, although he had once been a significant fighter. Thirty-five thousand people attended the fight in Houston, Texas.

'What's my name?'

Opposite: Ali's fight against Ernie Terrell at the beginning of 1967 got personal, in the way it had with Liston. Terrell refused to call Ali by his name, insisting on using his 'slave' name. It is said to have been the cruellest and most vicious fight of Ali's career. Early on in the fight, Terrell's vision became blurred because of an eye injury. Ali kept pounding away at Terrell until the fifteenth round, shouting 'What's my name?'

Above: Ali's treatment of Terrell invoked the anger of both the American press and the public. For a man who was considerate to most of his opponents, this display of savagery came at a terrible time. Soon after he was told to report for induction into the American armed forces.

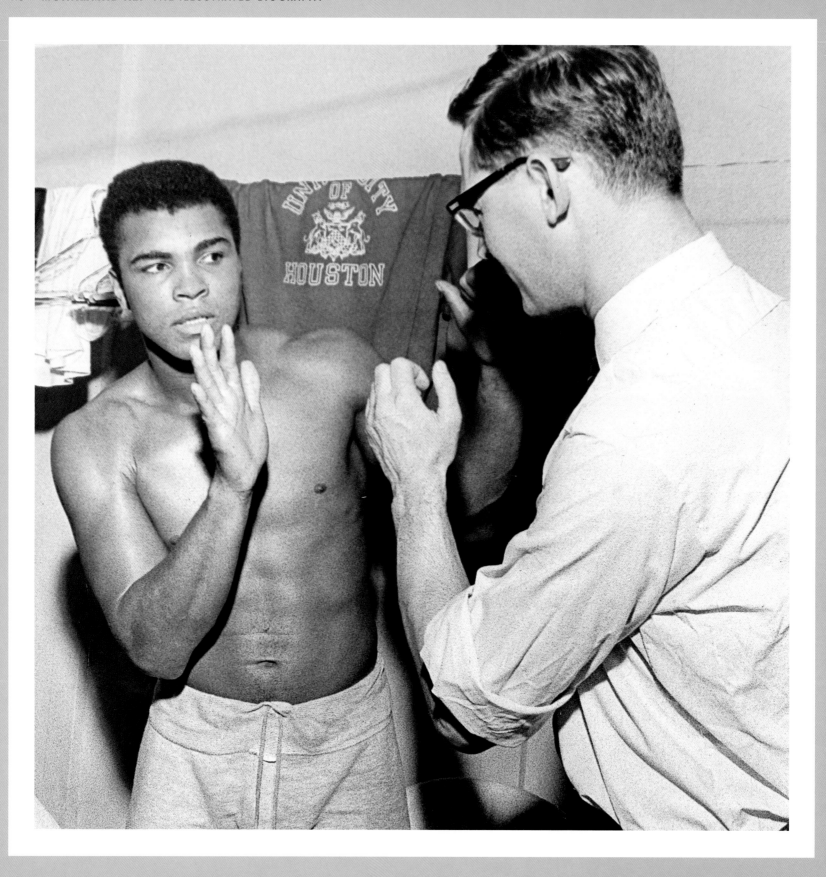

Knock out against Foley

Opposite: At a press
conference, Ali demonstrates
his strategy of defence before
the Terrell fight with British
journalist, Peter Moss. Terrell
was the most significant
challenger Ali had faced since
the last Liston fight.

Right: Ali was due to appear
for induction into the US army
in April. In March he fought a
new challenger at Madison
Square Garden in New York.
His opponent was Zora Folley,
whom Ali knocked out in the
seventh round. Folley said
later that the punch was so
fast, he hadn't seen it.

Forbidden to fight

Above: At the induction, Ali refused to step forward when his former name – Cassius Marcellus Clay – had been called. Public opinion was against him. Even before he was officially found guilty, the New York State Athletic Commission stripped him of his title and forbade him to fight in America. He was sentenced to five years' imprisonment (which he never served) and a $10,000 fine. His passport was taken away, which meant that he had no immediate means of earning a living. However, he loved to spar with local children outside his house in Miami.

Right: In 1971 Ali was on tour, sponsored by Ovaltine. He had been granted a licence to fight again in 1970 after three years out of the ring. He visited Nigeria, Italy, Switzerland and England.

Ali remarries

Right: Ali with his second wife Belinda. He had divorced Sonji in 1964, his reasons being that Sonji didn't dress according to the Islamic tenets Ali believed in and that were enforced by the Nation of Islam. He had been deeply in love with his first wife and chose his second carefully. Belinda was already involved with the Nation of Islam. They married soon after Ali was stripped of his title.

Left: English artist Sarah Leighton meets Ali in London for the first time in 1971. She begins preparations to paint his portrait.

Part Three

Back in the Ring

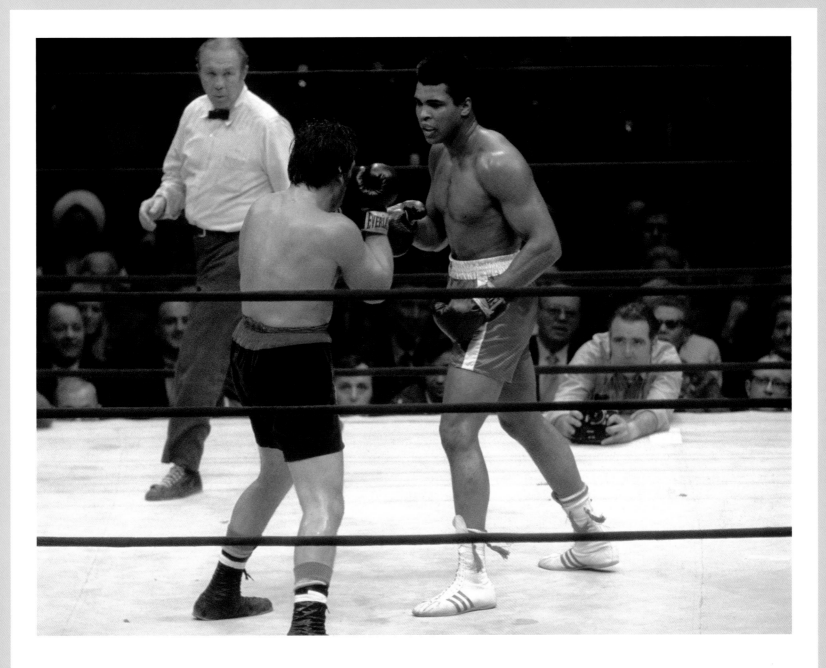

Return to the ring

Opposite: Ali's first fight on his return to boxing was against Jerry Quarry. A legal loophole meant that he could fight in the state of Georgia and the fight went ahead in Atlanta in October 1970. Ali was cautious about his chances, saying, 'It's been so long ... I'm fighting for my freedom.' He took a serious blow in the second round, but won the fight in the third when he opened a deep cut in Quarry's eye and the referee stopped the fight.

Above: Ali was victorious in his second fight after three years' absence from the boxing arena when he fought Oscar Bonavena in New York in December 1970. However, it was clear that he didn't have the level of fitness that had made him seem almost invincible in the previous decade. When Ali decided to return to boxing to earn his living, Elijah Muhammad cut him out for a year, but relaxed after it was clear that others in the movement stayed loyal to the boxer.

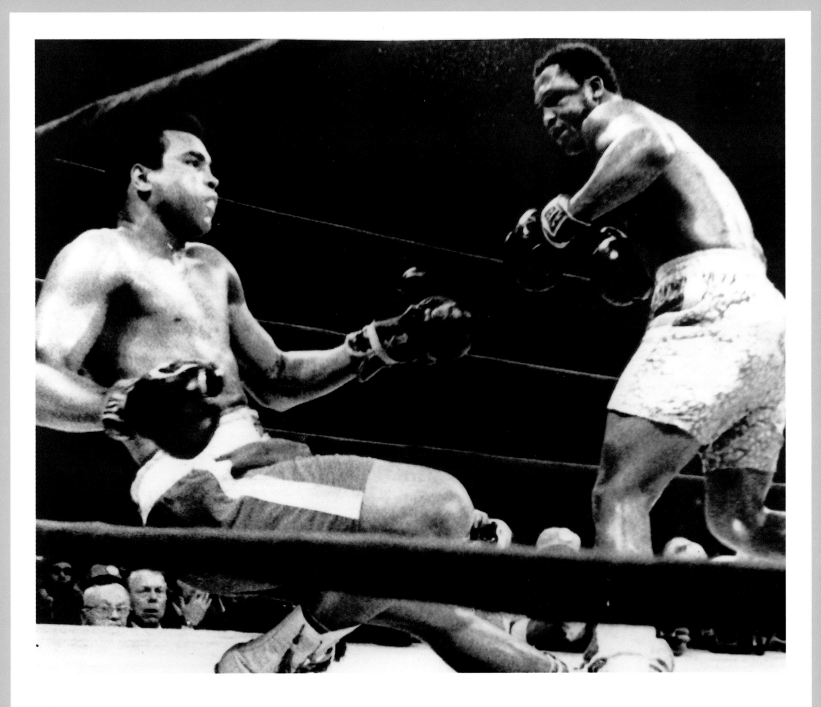

Ali loses to Frazier

Opposite: During Ali's absence from boxing, Joe Frazier had won the title of World Heavyweight Champion. Now a date was fixed for these two undefeated champions to fight – on March 8, 1971 at Madison Square Gardens, New York. This was the bout Ali needed to win.

Above: Ali put up a good fight, but Frazier began to land some heavy punches and although Ali rallied, he was knocked down by Frazier's left hook in the fifteenth round. Ali got up and staggered through to the end, but the bout went to Frazier. Ali was philosophical: 'Just lost a fight, that's all ... I'll probably be a better man for it.'

Police step in

Above: Crowds began to storm the ring after the fight. The police had to step in to prevent a riot. Ali was taken to hospital to have his jaw X-rayed. It wasn't broken, and Ali left the hospital against the advice of doctors. He didn't want to have to say that Frazier had put him in hospital. His pride might have been soothed by the phenomenal fee each fighter received – $2,500,000 a piece.

Opposite: Ali appeared as guest of honour at a dinner given by the World Sporting Club in London on October 18, 1971. His conviction had been overturned and his passport given back to him. Here he mock spars with Jack Bodell, at the time the British and Empire heavyweight champion.

Exhibition bouts

Above: Ali fought nearly 30 exhibition matches during 1971 and 1972, helping generate a considerable amount of income after spending three years outside the ring. Here he is pictured with Alonzo Johnson and Alan Burton. Ali was so impressed with Burton's performance on the night that he invited him to join his exhibition team.

Opposite: Johnny Frankham was the English Southern Area light heavyweight champion. Ali allowed himself to be toppled for the cameras.

Training with the family

Left: December 1971, Switzerland. Ali's twin daughters Rasheeda and Jamillah look slightly alarmed as their father incorporates pushing their pram into his training. He was due to fight German boxer Jürgen Blin on the 26th of the month. Blin was knocked out in seven rounds.

Opposite: In November 1972 Ali fought Bob Foster in Nevada. Ali knocked Foster out in the eighth round, but sustained a cut under his left eyebrow that needed stitches. The face that had remained unharmed in the sixties was beginning to feel the punches.

A visit to Dublin

Above: In July 1972 Ali visited Dublin, where he was to fight Al 'Blue' Lewis. The crowds at Croke Park look on as the greatest trains. Lewis had been in prison in 1968, and Ali had helped him by fighting some exhibition matches with him. On the night of the fight in Dublin, 7,000 fans literally gatecrashed the arena to watch. Ali knocked Lewis out in the eleventh round.

Opposite: Ali received three vicious punches from one of his sparring partners, Tony Doyle, while preparing for the fight against Joe Bugner in February 1973 in Nevada. The streak of cruelty in Ali was briefly on show when he said to the press that 'sparring partners are the lowest form of life'. When Doyle retaliated, 800 onlookers cheered.

Another defeat for Patterson

Above: Floyd Patterson and Ali met again in September 1972 at Madison Square Garden in New York. Ali's reflexes were not what they had been – he could no longer whip his head back as he had before he had been forced to stop boxing – but he nevertheless knocked Patterson out in the seventh round.

Opposite: Ali outside the Royal Lancaster Hotel in London, before leaving for Makkah. It was the first of many pilgrimages to Saudi Arabia, and over time, as Ali developed a deeper understanding of Islam, he said he was able to appreciate it more. Later this year he would become a father again – to a son, Muhammad Eban Ali, by Belinda and to a daughter Miya, by one of his girlfriends. After a faithful marriage to Sonji, Ali found fidelity the hardest of his marriage vows to keep.

In training for the Bugner fight

Right: Ali in training for the Bugner fight. The hammering by Doyle in the sparring session had raised questions among sportswriters and pundits. Bugner had disposed of Doyle in the previous year without much trouble at all.

Opposite: Ali before the Bugner fight. He had allowed members of the public to watch him train for a dollar a time. Ali wasn't as committed as he should have been to his training but nevertheless some of the sparring and training sessions were said to have been more exciting than the fight itself.

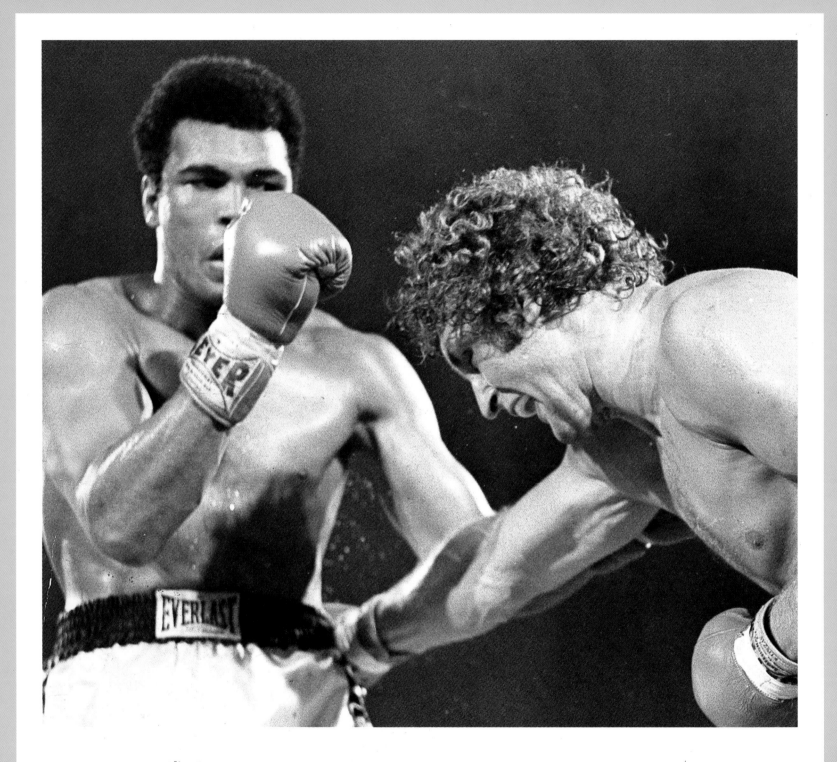

Ali v Bugner

Above and opposite: The fight, which took place on Valentine's Day in Las Vegas, was slow and dull. The odds in favour of Bugner were 8–1, so no one expected Ali to be defeated.

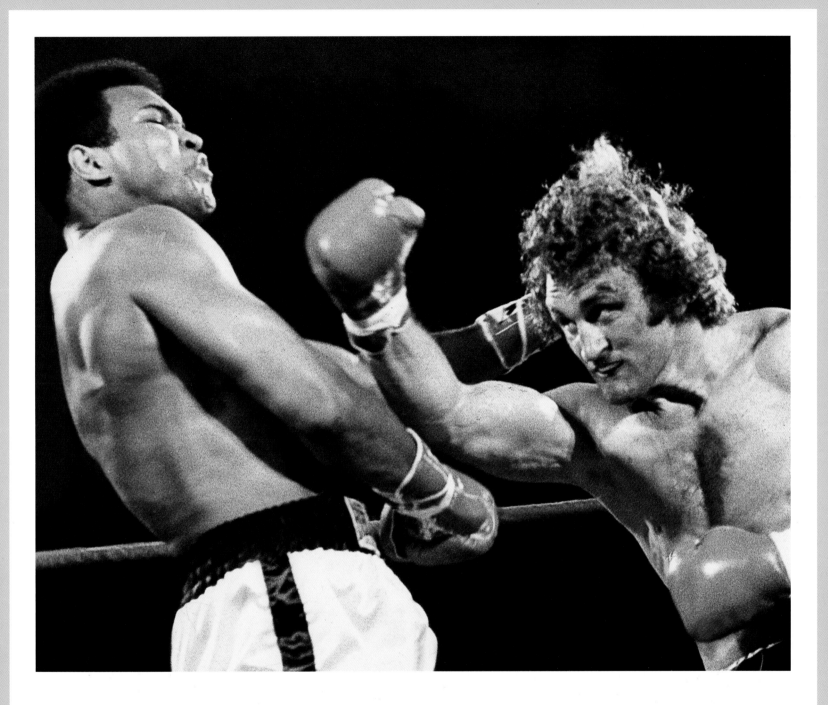

Tenth win since defeat by Frazier

Above and opposite: Ali's win over Bugner was his tenth since his defeat by Frazier in 1971, with knock-outs against Jimmy Ellis, Jurgen Blin, Jerry Quarry, Al Lewis, Floyd Patterson and Bob Foster. His next contest was against a relatively unknown boxer, Ken Norton, in six weeks' time. It wasn't expected to be a difficult fight. Again Ali didn't train enough and the ex-Marine Norton not only won after 12 rounds, but managed to break Ali's jaw in an early round. Ali fought on.

Preparing for a rematch with Norton

Opposite: Ali appears at a press conference for a rematch against Norton, which was set to take place on September 10, 1973. After the first Norton fight, he had undergone 90 minutes of surgery to fix his jaw and spent six months recuperating. He was philosophical about his previous defeat: 'too many easy victories can ruin a fighter just like a long line of defeats. You start thinking your name alone will win. You forget all the sacrifices that go into winning.' He started training harder.

Right: Ali was now in the best physical shape he had been in since his enforced retirement from boxing. He said of Norton, 'I took a nobody and created a monster. I gave him glory. Now I have to punish him bad.' Ali beat Norton in the twelfth round.

Realizing a dream

Opposite: Ali realized a long-held dream and opened his own training camp at Deer Lake, Pennsylvania. He modelled it on the camp of his first trainer, Archie Moore, with the names of great boxers painted on boulders. When he finally retired from boxing, he leased the premises for a dollar a year as a refuge for pregnant teenagers.

Right: Ali trained hard for a Frazier rematch due to take place at the beginning of 1974. Despite the fact that George Foreman had won the World Heavyweight title from Frazier, Ali nevertheless needed to prove he could beat Frazier on his way to regain the championship for himself.

Rematch with Frazier

Opposite: Days before the fight in Madison Square Garden, Ali and Frazier brawled on television, during a joint interview, when Frazier slipped in the fact that Ali had had to have surgery. The argument escalated, they were both fined $5,000, and the public interest in the fight reached fever pitch.

Above: The fight took place on January 28, 1974. Not all of Ali's opponents were able to take his comments as part of the publicity game and the ill feeling with Frazier ran deep. Despite this, it was an evenly matched game, with little viciousness, and Ali won in the twelfth round. Frazier immediately demanded a rematch.

Rumble in the jungle

Above and opposite: The fight between Ali and George Foreman took place in Kinshasa, Zaire, in 1974. President Mobutu Sese Seko, a formidable dictator, put up $10 million of his country's funds to host the fight. It became known as 'the rumble in the jungle'. Ali was immediately popular with Zaireans, Foreman less so (he had offended by arriving with an Alsatian dog, a symbol of colonial Belgian repression). Foreman suffered a serious cut to his eye during training and given that cancelling the fight would have bankrupted the country, both were 'encouraged' to stay until the fight could be staged on October 30. Foreman had the most powerful punch in the history of heavyweight boxing, but Ali managed to tire him out, absorbing his punches on the ropes rather than dancing out of the way, a technique later called 'rope-a-dope'. He finally knocked Foreman out in the eighth round.

Talking to the press

Left: Ali at a press conference in Kinshasa before the fight. Ali had (unlike Foreman) brought a huge entourage, who were accommodated in luxury and Don King, the fight promoter, had intended to tie the match in with a music festival, at which the great James Brown and BB King would perform. In the end, the fight was postponed, taking place long after the festival.

Opposite: Ali came to London, where he intended to see the fight between Joe Bugner and American Boone Kirkman at the Royal Albert Hall. Here at a press conference, he was welcomed with warmth and admiration. His stand against the American government was seen as a brave act; and his victory over Foreman had made him once again the main contender.

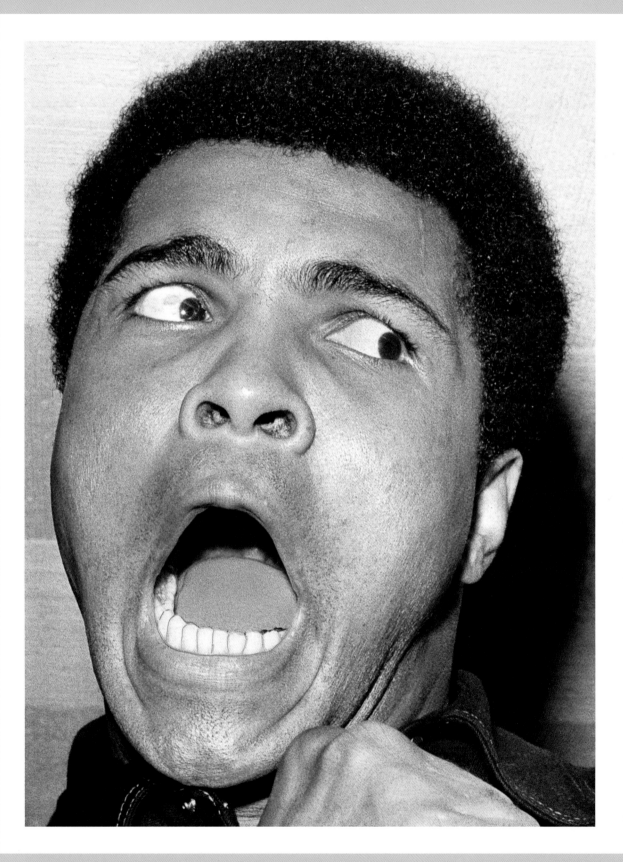

A tempting offer

Left: The old Ali is back, giving the press and public what they want during his five-day visit to London in 1974. Before the Foreman fight, Ali had said it would be his last. Now he said he would go on until 'somebody is great enough to beat me'.

Opposite: Ali puts on a fighting pose after news that he has been offered $15 million to fight Foreman and Frazier together – Frazier first over ten rounds, then Foreman without a rest. The money would be divided equally between the three. It would be enough to retire on.

A warm reception

Opposite: Ali gave a 'talk-in' at London's New Victoria Theatre. It was chaired by Reg Gutteridge, the best boxing writer on Fleet Street. When Ali came down into the orchestra pit to sign autographs, the audience went wild and the event became a crush. One girl fainted and several injuries were sustained. Ali, unnerved by this level of hysteria, slipped out of the stage door unnoticed.

Above: On Ali's right is Paddy Monaghan, the champion's biggest British fan. He was once an amateur welterweight and ran Ali's British fan club full-time and unpaid. He was loyal when the press and public turned against Ali over his political stance and when they were ready to write him off after the first Frazier fight.

A friendly left hook

Above: Joe Bugner greets Ali with a friendly left hook outside the Dominion Theatre in London's Tottenham Court Road. Bugner wanted an attempt at the world title and a fight was scheduled for the following year. Bugner was due to fight American Boone Kirkman; Ali intended to watch as he too was going to fight Kirkman.

Opposite: Ali made a speech at the Anglo-American Sporting Club's dinner held in his honour at the London Hilton during his brief visit in December 1974. After the dinner Ali met the staff in the kitchen and gave the chef a friendly warning.

Contest in Kuala Lumpur

Opposite: Ali and Bugner fought in Kuala Lumpur in Malaysia on June 30, 1975. Ali had not been committed enough in training during the run-up to the fight, but just days before picked up the pace by sparring for 15 rounds against two partners. The climate was stiflingly humid and it played against Bugner, who went the full 15 rounds but lost to Ali. Ali earned $2 million and began talking of retiring.

Above Ali and British light-heavyweight boxer John Conteh discuss boxing for BBC radio.

Thriller in Manila

Above: Ali met Frazier in the ring for the third time in Manila in 1975 . Again, Ali wound Frazier up and the latter did not take Ali's banter cordially – it often overstepped the mark. Ali seemed to control the fight in the early rounds but Frazier came back in the middle of the bout. In the end, Ali won in 14 rounds, having caused Frazier's eye to swell so badly that he couldn't see properly. Ali retained the title, but later he said to Dundee that in the middle of the fight – when Frazier pummelled Ali with his notorious left hooks – it was the closest he'd come to dying. Again Ali started to discuss retiring.

Opposite: Ali clowns for the cameras, this time looking surprised to see a story about himself in the newspaper.

The Greatest

Opposite and right: In 1976 Ali came to London to promote his book, *The Greatest*, a biography that had been written by Richard Durham, with Ali's involvement. The press conference was held at the Savoy hotel, one of many publicity events to promote the book. These included books signings that were mobbed by adoring fans. The press were told to stick to the subject of the book and not the subject of Ali's marriage to Belinda, which was coming to a bruising end. The book was an instant bestseller.

Ali's new love

Opposite: Ali on his latest London visit, with his spiritual mentor Jeremiah Shabazz and this younger brother. Clearly they turned a blind eye to Ali openly travelling with Veronica Porche ('Ali's other wife') despite still being married to Belinda.

Above: Ali fought Jimmy Young in Washington in March 1976. Ali tried to add some spice before the proceedings, but the match proved to be a near-interminable 15 rounds. Dundee himself talked with distaste of Ali's victory over his outclassed opponent: 'It was horrible, it was a nightmare … But I don't think Ali will take anyone so cheaply again.'

Getting back in shape

Opposite: Ali knew he had been out of shape for the Young fight – he had weighed 230 lbs (21 lbs heavier than his opponent) – and the press commentary on the fight had been less than complimentary. He was due to fight Britain's Richard Dunn in Munich in May 1976 and took his training much more seriously with this criticism in mind.

Right: Ali watches Dunn train, and playfully imitates Frankenstein's monster to put him off. Dunn continued sparring.

Ticket sales slow

Opposite: Ali and Dunn met and talked cordially before the fight. Ticket sales for the fight were very poor, not helped by the steep price of the tickets. Ali took a cut in pay for 2,000 tickets, which were offered to American military personnel serving in Germany – a rapprochement given Ali's history with the American army.

Above: Ali had trained to a high level for this match – to such an extent that he announced he would be happy to take on the winner of a forthcoming Frazier–Foreman fight. All talk of retirement seemed to have been forgotten.

A strong start by Dunn

Opposite and above: Dunn had lost too much weight days before the fight and so stopped training to gain it again. He came out in the first round fighting hard and managed to land some strong right punches. In the third round, Ali began to retaliate with determination, and though he kept knocking Dunn down (he had said, 'Dunn is going to get done!'), the Briton kept trying to come back.

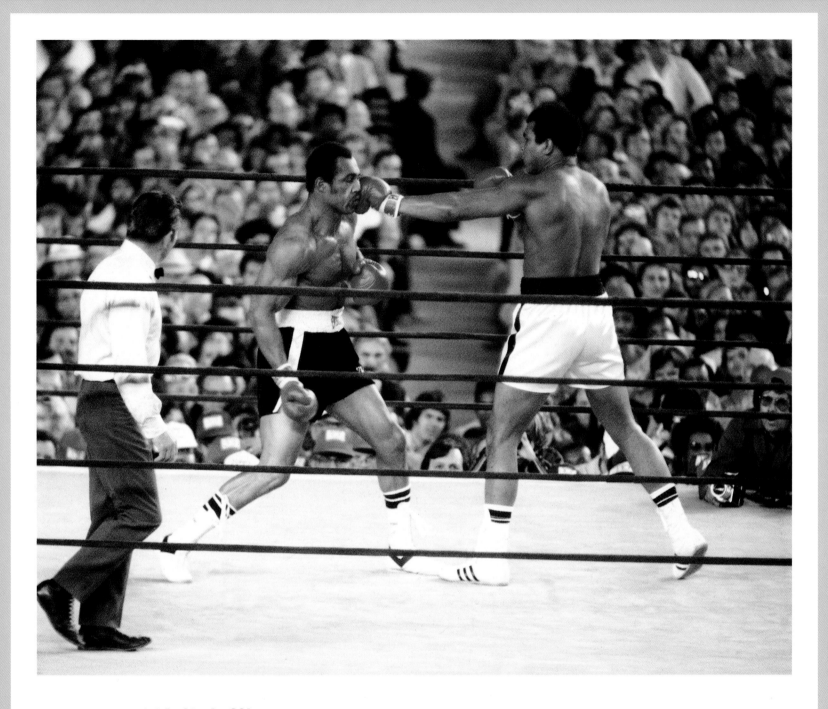

Finished in the fifth

Opposite: Finally the referee counted Dunn out in the fifth round, awarding a technical knock-out to Ali. In the audience were some glamorous names of the time, including Prince Rainier and Princess Grace of Monaco, and Elizabeth Taylor, the woman who had famously distracted Ali in an early fight against Henry Cooper.

Above: Ali's third fight against Ken Norton took place in September 1976.

Starring in a bio-pic

Left and opposite: The actress Annette Chase played Belinda in a film of Ali's life, *The Greatest*, released by Columbia Pictures. Ali starred as himself, as did many of his entourage. Although he was very entertaining, the film itself did not receive much critical acclaim.

Beginning to tire

Opposite and above: Proof that Ali was beginning to tire came in a fight against Spain's Alfredo Evangelista in May 1977. Seven months previously Ali had taken on Ken Norton once again. Ali won but Norton felt the victory had gone to Ali unfairly. Norton complained, 'I was robbed. I won ten rounds, at least nine.' Unlike Norton, Evangelista was not a serious contender. Nevertheless, Ali was not able to finish the bout off early and the fight went on for 15 rounds. Commentators agreed the match was slow and boring, and a considerable proportion of the 12,000 fans in the audience must have at last seen that Ali was past his best. The journalist Howard Cosell called it 'one of the worst fights ever fought'.

A new chapter in family life

Opposite: Ali came to London in 1977 to attend the British premiere of his film, *The Greatest*. Among many other appearances, Ali was a guest on the DJ Pete Murray's BBC Radio show, *Open House*. Ali and Belinda were finally divorced and Ali had married his girlfriend Veronica Porche.

Above: Ali and Veronica had had a daughter Hana the previous year. Ali took Hana to a press conference. After she started crying, Ali gave her a bottle and continued his discussion with assembled journalists. Ali managed to keep off the subject he was there to promote – his film, *The Greatest* – and launched into a discussion of world peace.

A special award

Opposite and left: During his London visit to promote the film, Ali was given an award by the Victoria Sporting Club. Ali's physician resigned two months after this, when he saw the state of his friend after a fight against Earnie Shavers. This articulate and loyal doctor had been with Ali from the early days but saw it as immoral to continue encouraging Ali into the ring.

No longer the prettiest

Opposite: The British press were bowled over by little Hana and declared that she, not her father, was now 'the prettiest'.

Above: Ali always gave the public attention and was generous in his support for good causes. He visited one of London's children's hospital, Great Ormond Street, and here talks to eight-year-old Jason Baker and his nurse. Ali would often talk to children when out and about among the public.

A subdued Ali

Opposite and above: Ali and Veronica. In February 1978 Ali fought Leon Spinks, a maverick young boxer 12 years his junior. Spinks was an Olympic gold medallist but had fought few professional fights. Ali did not prepare himself well enough and for the first time, lost the title in the last round. Soon after a subdued Ali and Veronica stop off in London on their way to Bangladesh, where Ali is made Honorary Consul General (opposite). A rematch against Spinks was finally scheduled after wranglings involving the ever more powerful Don King. A few years previously he had tried to entice Ali away from Herbert Muhammad, but Ali remained loyal.

Ali announces his retirement

Opposite: The return match against Spinks took place in New Orleans in September 1978. During training, Ali said, 'All the time I'm in pain ... I hate it, but I know this is my last fight.' The fight was slow but Spinks had not trained properly and Ali kept away from the ropes. Ali won the fight and regained his title. Nine months later he retired for the first time.

Above: In June 1978 Ali had gone on a 12-day goodwill tour of Moscow, Tashkent and Samarkand. He took part in some exhibition fights and charmed Muscovites queuing to see Lenin's tomb by jogging around Red Square. Here he prays in a mosque in Tashkent.

Travelling with the family

Opposite and above: In March 1978 Ali and Veronica had another daughter, Laila. They often took their children with them on tour. On this occasion, Ali, world champion once again, had brought his family back to London to record a television interview.

'I'm in the worst shape in the world.'

Opposite: In May 1979 Ali participates in a five-round exhibition fight with British heavyweight champion John L Gardener in London. He now wore protective head gear in exhibitions. He was increasingly overweight, even admitting to watching journalists, 'I'm in the worst shape in the world.' He announced that he would be retiring in six weeks.

Above: In London in 1980, Ali lends some publicity to fellow boxer and friend John Conteh, who has just opened a restaurant. Throughout his career, Ali had been generous almost to a fault. This generosity benefited some deserving cases and others not so deserving, and he often attracted characters who took advantage of his good nature. Despite having retired, and earning money endorsing various products (including Toyota), bad financial management and exploitation led him back into the ring to earn more money – a decision that may have cost him his long-term health.

Back in the ring

Left and opposite: Ali kept out of the ring for two years but it drew him back whether for financial reasons or because he missed it. His first major fight, after an injury during training, was against Larry Holmes, who had taken the title from Ken Norton in 1978. Holmes wasn't keen, saying Ali should stay in retirement, but Ali was determined. One of the main instigators of the Holmes match was Don King, who would very soon control the lion's share of world boxing.

SHOWTIME
NAME TO
The Louisiana Superdome,
Largest Enclosed Stadium
EXTRA
The New Orleans Times
TUBBS WINS
PRO FIGHT!
LLOYD
GOES
ELLIS
DECLARED
DISCO QUEEN

Holmes fight halted in the tenth

Left: Ali hugs his beloved Hana before the Holmes fight.

Opposite: Just before the fight Ali was diagnosed with a medical condition and given drugs that had a detrimental effect at least on his short-term health. He became dehydrated and exhausted, but pushed through this during the bout. Holmes was in control of the fight, but Ali kept going. It was Dundee, Ali's loyal henchman, who told the referee to stop the fight in the tenth round.

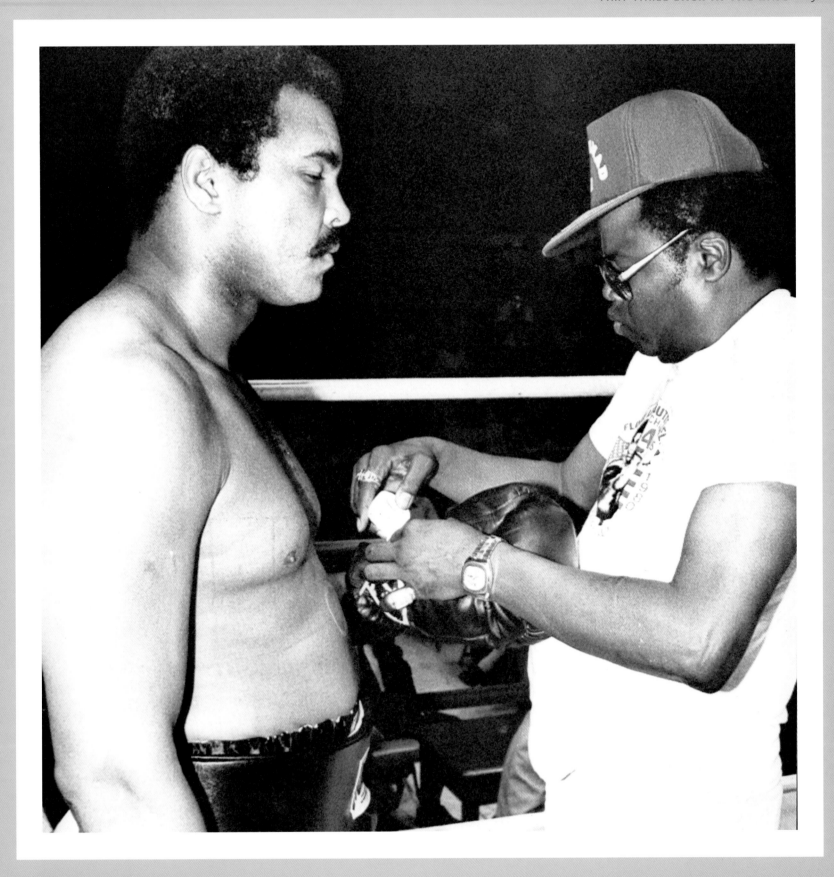

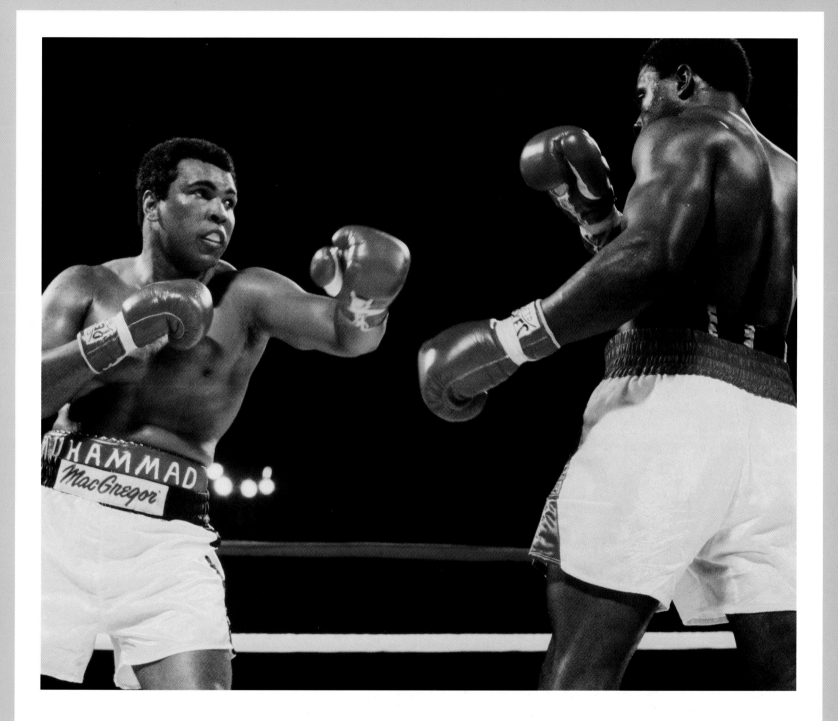

Final contest

Opposite and above: The greatest was tempted back into the ring for what would be his last fight against Trevor Berbick at the end of December 1981. The fight was a walkover – Ali had lost all speed and Berbick was young and fit. Ali was philosophical about his loss: 'I know it's the end; I'm not crazy ... but at least I didn't go down. We all lose sometimes. We all grow old.'

Part Four

I'm Just
Getting Started

Just getting started

Above: Ali is as obliging as ever to his fans, who ask for his autograph at Heathrow airport. Ali didn't view the end of his boxing career as the end of his public life. In a later interview he said, 'People say I had a full life, but I ain't dead yet. I'm just getting started, fighting injustice, fighting racism, fighting crime, fighting illiteracy, fighting poverty, using this face the world knows so well and going out and fighting for truth and different causes.'

Opposite: After his defeat by Holmes, Ali was back in London promoting *Freedom Road*, a TV mini-series in which he appeared with American actor Kris Kristofferson. It was a hit but it couldn't pay him what he could earn through boxing.

A connection with the past

Above: At the press reception for *Freedom Road* at the Dorchester hotel in London, Ali meets Tony Madigan, who had competed at the 1960 Rome Olympics where Ali had won his gold medal. Madigan was now a journalist for *The Australian*.

Opposite: Ali greets one of his younger fans. As the father of nine children, Maryum, Jamillah, Rasheeda, Muhammad Ali Jr, Hana, Leila, Miya, Khaliah and an adopted son, Asaad, Ali was well used to conversing with children.

Involved in a scandal

Opposite: Ali and Veronica pose for cameras. At home, a scandal was revealed involving Harold Smith, one of Ali's associates, who had used Ali's name to raise funds for an organization intended to protect fighters when they turned professional. Ironically, Harold Smith exploited the very fighter who had made this possible by embezzling funds to the tune of $21 million.

Above: Ali meets Freddie Starr, an English comedian known as the 'Mersey Mouth, Parkinson let the two 'loudmouths' riff for two hours, and the highlights were broadcast in January 1981.

Diagnosed with Parkinson's syndrome

Opposite and above: In 1984 Muhammad Ali was diagnosed with Parkinson's syndrome, a non-progressive relative of Parkinson's disease. Almost overnight, Ali had turned into an old man, walking slowly, losing coordination, and slurring his speech. However, with medication, these symptoms almost vanished. His condition was, in fact, diagnosed later as Parkinson's disease. In that year, depsite his poor health, Ali came to England to open a multi-racial centre in inner-city Birmingham.

Marriage in difficulty

Above: After retiring, Ali moved to Los Angeles with Veronica and the children. However, they still travelled a great deal. Ali found it difficult to adjust to his new life and his marriage to Veronica ran into trouble. They eventually divorced in 1986.

Opposite: Since his conversion to Islam in the 1960s, his faith has been a constant feature of Ali's life. He spends a great deal of time studying Islam, reading the Qur'an and signing Islamic texts in an effort to propagate his faith.

Magician

Opposite and right: The previous year, the press had rushed to say that Ali had brain damage, but on this occasion in 1984, with his new medication, he was on his old form again. Here he entertains journalists in his hotel suite with magic tricks, bringing down on his head the condemnation of the Magic Circle when he revealed on television how the tricks were done.

Retaining an interest

Left: London, 1986. Although retired Ali retains an interest in boxing. Here he is pictured with promoter Don King arriving in London for the title fight between Britain's Frank Bruno and the world heavyweight champion Tim Witherspoon.

Opposite: Ali visits Tim Witherspoon at his training camp in Basildon, Essex.

Marriage to Lonnie

Opposite: Since the early eighties, Ali had been friends with Lonnie Williams, who had known him since she was a child. After Ali's divorce from Veronica, they married, and Lonnie began to care for him and to straighten out his business affairs, which for years had been in disarray through neglect and exploitation of Ali's good nature.

Right: With Henry Cooper. The two old adversaries meet at the British launch of Thomas Hauser's biography of Ali. Despite his retirement from the sport, the crowds are no thinner than they have been on previous visits, and Ali is mobbed at a later book signing.

Reunited

Opposite and above: Ali is reunited with two of his most formidable opponents, Joe Frazier and George Foreman, to promote a video, *Champions Forever*, showcasing Ali's greatest fighting moments. Despite appearances, Frazier never forgave Ali for his comments, though Ali apologized: 'I'm sorry I hurt him; Joe Frazier is a good man.' Foreman had had a difficult journey after his defeat, and said generously of Ali: 'I realized I had lost to a great champion who transcended the sport of boxing, and that I should be proud to have been a big chapter in his legendary career.'

Bringing some comfort

Opposite: While in London, Ali visited Michael Watson in hospital. Watson was a British boxer who had gone into a coma after a fight with another British contender, Chris Eubank. Ali had asked permission to visit, and was of course welcomed with open arms. Ali has his arm around Watson's mother's shoulder, and they are both flanked by the grown-up twins, Rasheeda and Jamillah. Watson rallied after the great man's visit.

Right: In 1993 Geoffrey C Ewing starred in Ali, a one-man show about the boxer's life, at the Mermaid Theatre in London's West End. The actor and the eponymous hero share a joke. Ali attended a special charity performance.

Best of friends

Above: A warm handshake for Ali from Henry Cooper. Ali is accompanied by Howard Bingham, his closest and most longstanding friend. Bingham has also been Ali's principal photographer. Ali has said of Bingham, 'I have the best friend in the world, and that's Howard Bingham. He never asks for anything; he's always there when someone needs him.' Ali rarely voices his disappointment at how other 'friends' have taken advantage of him.

Opposite: Ali visited London again to promote another book, *Muhammad Ali: A 30 Year Journey*. He still needed to earn his living promoting the legend, as nearly all the millions he had earned over the years had disappeared. On this occasion he took the time to visit Henry Cooper's gym on the Old Kent Road in south-east London.

Sportsman of the century

Above: After a few years out of the public eye, Ali returned with a magnificent gesture. Despite the obvious deterioration in his health over the intervening years, in 1996 he lit the Olympic torch for the Atlanta games. His return inspired compassion and admiration. Here in 1999 he is in London to receive an award, and take the time to visit adoring fans in Brixton.

Opposite: David Beckham meets Muhammad Ali at the BBC Sportsman of the Year award in 1999. In the same month Ali was named 'Sportsman of the Century' by *Sports Illustrated*, a just achievement for this unique figure of the twentieth century.

Professional Fight Chronology

1960

| 29 Oct | Tunney Hunsaker | Freedom Hall, Louisville, Kentucky | Win R6 |
| 27 Dec | Herb Siler | Auditorium, Miami Beach, Florida | KO R4 |

1961

17 Jan	Tony Esperti	Auditorium, Miami Beach, Florida	KO R3
07 Feb	Jim Robinson	Convention Hall, Miami Beach, Florida	KO R1
21 Feb	Donnie Fleeman	Convention Hall, Miami Beach, Florida	KO R7
19 Apr	Lamar Clark	Freedom Hall, Louisville, Kentucky	KO R2
26 Jun	Duke Sabedon	Convention Center, Las Vegas, Nevada	Win R10
22 Jul	Alonzo Johnson	Freedom Hall, Louisville, Kentucky	Win R10
07 Oct	Alex Miteff	Freedom Hall, Louisville, Kentucky	KO R6
29 Nov	Willi Besmanoff	Freedom Hall, Louisville, Kentucky	KO R7

1962

19 Feb	Sonny Banks	Madison Square Garden, New York City	KO R4
28 Mar	Don Warner	Convention Hall, Miami Beach, Florida	KO R4
23 Apr	George Logan	Memorial Sports Arena, Los Angeles	KO R6
19 May	Billy Daniels	St Nicholas Arena, New York City	KO R7
20 Jul	Alejandro Lavorante	Memorial Sports Arena, Los Angeles	KO R5
15 Nov	Archie Moore	Memorial Sports Arena, Los Angeles	KO R4

1963

24 Jan	Charlie Powell	Civic Arena, Pittsburgh, Pennsylvania	KO R3
13 Mar	Doug Jones	Madison Square Garden, New York City	Win R10
18 Jun	Henry Cooper	Wembley Stadium, London, England	KO R5

1964

| 25 Feb | Sonny Liston | Convention Hall, Miami Beach, Florida (Wins World Heavyweight Title) | KO R7 |

1965

25 May	Sonny Liston	St Dominic's Arena, Lewiston, ME (Retains World Heavyweight Title)	KO R1
31 Jul	Jimmy Ellis	San Juan, PR	Exhibition R3
31 Jul	Cody Jones	San Juan, PR	Exhibition R3
16 Aug	Cody Jones	Goteborg, Sweden	Exhibition R2
16 Aug	Jimmy Ellis	Goteborg, Sweden	Exhibition R2
20 Aug	Jimmy Ellis	London, England	Exhibition R4
20 Aug	Cody Jones	Paisley, Scotland	Exhibition R4
22 Nov	Floyd Patterson	Convention Center, Las Vegas (Retains World Heavyweight Title)	KO R12

1966

29 Mar	George Chuvalo	Maple Leaf Gardens, Toronto, Canada (Retains World Heavyweight Title)	Win R15
21 May	Henry Cooper	Highbury Stadium, London, England (Retains World Heavyweight Title)	KO6
06 Aug	Brian London	Earls Court Stadium, London, England (Retains World Heavyweight Title)	KO3
10 Sep	Karl Mildenberger	Wald Stadium, Frankfurt, Germany (Retains World Heavyweight Title)	KO12
14 Nov	Cleveland Williams	Astrodome, Houston, Texas (Retains World Heavyweight Title)	KO R3

1969

06 Feb	Ernie Terrell	Astrodome, Houston, Texas (Retains World Heavyweight Title)	Win R15
22 Mar	Zora Folley	Madison Square Garden, New York City (Retains World Heavyweight Title)	KO R7
15 Jun	Alvin Lewis	Detroit, Michigan	Exhibition R3
15 Jun	Orvill Qualls	Detroit, Michigan	Exhibition R3

1970

Sep	3 opponents	Morehouse College, Atlanta, Georgia	Exhibition
26 Oct	Jerry Quarry	Municipal Auditorium, Atlanta, Georgia	KO R3
07 Dec	Oscar Bonavena	Madison Square Garden, New York City	KO R15

1971

08 Mar	Joe Frazier	Madison Square Garden, New York City (For World Heavyweight Title)	Lost R15
25 Jun	J.D. McCauley	Dayton, Ohio	Exhibition R2
25 Jun	Eddie Brooks	Dayton, Ohio	Exhibition R3
25 Jun	Rufus Brassell	Dayton, Ohio	Exhibition R3
30 Jun	Alex Mack	Charleston, SC	Exhibition R3
30 Jun	Eddie Brooks	Charleston, SC	Exhibition R4
26 Jul	Jimmy Ellis	Astrodome, Houston, Texas	KO R12
21 Aug	Lancer Johnson	Caracas	Exhibition R4
21 Aug	Eddie Brooks	Caracas	Exhibition R4
23 Aug	Lancer Johnson	Port of Spain	Exhibition R4
23 Aug	Eddie Brooks	Port of Spain	Exhibition R2
06 Nov	James Summerville	Buenos Aires	Exhibition R5
06 Nov	Miguel Paez	Buenos Aires	Exhibition R5
17 Nov	Buster Mathis	Astrodome, Houston, Texas	Win R12
26 Dec	Jürgen Blin	Hallenstadion Arena, Zurich, Switzerland	KO R7

1972

01 Apr	Mac Foster	Martial Arts Hall, Tokyo, Japan	Win R15
01 May	George Chuvalo	Pacific Coliseum, Vancouver, Canada	Win R12
27 Jun	Jerry Quarry	Convention Center, Las Vegas, Nevada	KO R7
01 Jul	Lonnie Bennett	Los Angeles, California	Exhibition R2
01 Jul	Eddie Jones	Los Angeles, California	Exhibition R2
01 Jul	Billy Ryan	Los Angeles, California	Exhibition R2
01 Jul	Charley James	Los Angeles, California	Exhibition R2
01 Jul	Rudy Clay	Los Angeles, California	Exhibition R2
19 Jul	Al Lewis	Croke Park, Dublin, Ireland	KO R11
24 Aug	Obie English	Baltimore, MD	Exhibition R4
24 Aug	Ray Anderson	Baltimore, MD	Exhibition R2
24 Aug	Alonzo Johnson	Baltimore, MD	Exhibition R2
24 Aug	George Hill	Baltimore, MD	Exhibition R2
28 Aug	Alonzo Johnson	Cleveland, Ohio	Exhibition R2
28 Aug	Amos Johnson	Cleveland, Ohio	Exhibition R2
28 Aug	Terry Daniels	Cleveland, Ohio	Exhibition R2
20 Sep	Floyd Patterson	Madison Square Garden, New York City	KO R7
11 Oct	John Dennis	Boston, Massachusetts	Exhibition R2
11 Oct	Cliff McDonald	Boston, Massachusetts	Exhibition R2
11 Oct	Doug Kirk	Boston, Massachusetts	Exhibition R2
11 Oct	Ray Anderson	Boston, Massachusetts	Exhibition R2
11 Oct	Paul Raymond	Boston, Massachusetts	Exhibition R2
21 Nov	Bob Foster	High Sierra Theater, Stateline, Nevada	KO R8

1973

14 Feb	Joe Bugner	Convention Center, Las Vegas, Nevada	Win R12
31 Mar	Ken Norton	Sports Arena, San Diego, California	Lost R12
10 Sep	Ken Norton	Forum, Inglewood, California	Win R12
20 Oct	Rudi Lubbers	Senyan Stadium, Jakarta, Indonesia	Win R12

1974

28 Jan	Joe Frazier	Madison Square Garden, New York City	Win R12
30 Oct	George Foreman	20th May Stadium, Kinshasa, Zaire (Wins World Heavyweight Title) KO R8	

1975

24 Mar	Chuck Wepner	Coliseum, Cleveland, Ohio (Retains World Heavyweight Title) KO R15	
16 May	Ron Lyle	Convention Center, Las Vegas, Nevada (Retains World Heavyweight Title) KO R11	
30 Jun	Joe Bugner	Merdeka Stadium, Kuala Lumpur, Malaysia (Retains World Heavyweight Title) Win R15	
01 Oct	Joe Frazier	Araheta Coliseum, Manila (Retains World Heavyweight Title) KO R14	

1976

20 Feb	Jean-Pierre Coopman	Clemente Coliseum, San Juan, Puerto Rico (Retains World Heavyweight Title) KO R5	
30 Apr	Jimmy Young	Capital Center, Landover, Maryland (Retains World Heavyweight Title) Win R15	
24 May	Richard Dunn	Olympiahalle, Munich, Germany (Retains World Heavyweight Title) KO R5	
25 Jun	Antonio Inoki	Tokyo, Japan	Exhibition D15
28 Sep	Ken Norton	Yankee Stadium, New York City (Retains World Heavyweight Title) Win R15	

1977

29 Jan	Peter Fuller	Boston, Massachusetts	Exhibition R4
29 Jan	Walter Haines	Boston, Massachusetts	Exhibition R1
29 Jan	Jerry Houston	Boston, Massachusetts	Exhibition R2
29 Jan	Ron Drinkwater	Boston, Massachusetts	Exhibition R2
29 Jan	Matt Ross	Boston, Massachusetts	Exhibition R2
29 Jan	Frank Smith	Boston, Massachusetts	Exhibition R1
16 May	Alfredo Evangelista	Capital Center, Landover, Maryland (Retains World Heavyweight Title) Win R15	
29 Sep	Earnie Shavers	Madison Square Garden, New York City (Retains World Heavyweight Title) Win R15	
02 Dec	Scott LeDoux	Chicago, Illinois	Exhibition R5

1979

15 Feb	Leon Spinks	Las Vegas Hilton, Las Vegas, Nevada (Lost World Heavyweight Title) Lost R15	
15 Sep	Leon Spinks	Superdome, New Orleans, Louisiana (Won World Heavyweight Title) Win R15	

1980

02 Oct	Larry Holmes	Caesar's Palace, Las Vegas, Nevada (For World Heavyweight Title) Lost R11	

1981

11 Dec	Trevor Berbick	QEII Sports Centre, Nassau, Bahamas	Lost R10

Acknowledgments

The photographs used in this book are from the archives of the *Daily Mail*.
Additional photographs to complete this celebration of the life of
Muhammed Ali have been provided by Getty Images.

Particular thanks to Steve Torrington and Alan Pinnock, without whose help
this book would not have been possible.

Courtesy Getty Images: pages 10, 17, 19, 20, 36, 42, 45, 48, 55, 80, 85, 119, 122, 131, 143, 169, 193